PRE-APPRENTICESHIP
MATHS & LITERACY FOR
HAIRDRESSING
Graduated exercises and practice exam

Andrew Spencer

A+ National Pre-apprenticeship Maths & Literacy for Hairdressing
1st Edition
Andrew Spencer

Publishing editors: Jane Moylan and Jana Raus
Editor: Kerry Nagle
Senior designer: Vonda Pestana
Cover designer: Vonda Pestana
Text designer: Vonda Pestana
Cover image: © Cengage Learning
Photo researcher: UC Publishing
Production controller: Jo Vraca & Damian Almeida
Reprint: Katie McCappin
Typeset by UC Publishing Pty Ltd

Any URLs contained in this publication were checked for currency during the production process. Note, however, that the publisher cannot vouch for the ongoing currency of URLs.

Acknowledgements
We would like to thank the following for permission to reproduce copyright material:

iStockphotos: p2 adisa, p4MistikaS, p5 powerofforever, p9 pixelbrat, p10 craftvision, p11 ivanmateev, p12 Floortje, p13 carollphoto, p15 thebroker, p16 muratsen, p17 iconogenic, p19 Deklofenak, p20 arenacreative, p22 Alija, p24 ivanmateev, p25 webphotographeer, p28 top left DSGpro, p28 bottom right TimMcClean, p30 sophielouise.

The publisher would like to acknowledge and thank the front cover models (Teagan Cousins , Vicky Karamanis and Aynslie Harper) for their involvement and co-operation. The publisher would also like to acknowledge and thank the East Malvern Masci Hair and Spa for allowing us to conduct the front cover photo shoot in the salon and for the staff assistance on the day.

For product information and technology assistance,
in Australia call 1300 790 853;
in New Zealand call 0800 449 725

For permission to use material from this text or product, please email aust.permissions@cengage.com

ISBN 978 0 17 046283 9

Cengage Learning Australia
Level 7, 80 Dorcas Street
South Melbourne, Victoria Australia 3205

Cengage Learning New Zealand
Unit 4B Rosedale Office Park
331 Rosedale Road, Albany, North Shore 0632, NZ

For learning solutions, visit cengage.com.au

Printed in Australia by Ligare Pty Limited.
1 2 3 4 5 6 7 25 24 23 22 21

A+ National
PRE-APPRENTICESHIP
Maths & Literacy for Hairdressing

Contents

Introduction

It has always been important to understand, from a teacher's perspective, the nature of the mathematical skills students need for their future, rather than teaching them textbook mathematics. This has been a guiding principle behind the development of the content in this workbook. To teach maths that is *relevant* to students seeking apprenticeships is the best that we can do, to give students an education in the field that they would like to work in.

The content in this resource is aimed at the level that is needed for a student to have the best possibility of improving their maths and literacy skills specifically for trades. Students can use this workbook to prepare for an apprenticeship entry assessment, or even to assist with basic numeracy and literacy at the VET/TAFE level. Coupled with the NelsonNet website, https://www.nelsonnet.com.au/free-resources, these resources have the potential to improve the students' understanding of basic mathematical concepts that can be applied to trades. These resources have been trialled, and they work.

Commonly used trade terms are introduced so that students have a basic understanding of terminology they will encounter in the workplace environment. Students who can complete this workbook and reach an 80 per cent or higher outcome in all topics will have achieved the goal of this resource. These students will go on to complete work experience, do a VET accredited course, or be able to gain entry into VET/TAFE or an apprenticeship in the trade of their choice.

The content in this workbook is the first step towards bridging the gap between what has been learnt in previous years, and what needs to be remembered and re-learnt for use in trades. Students will significantly benefit from the consolidation of the basic maths and literacy concepts.

Every school has students who want to work with their hands, and not all students want to go to university. The best students want to learn what they don't know, and if students want to learn, then this book has the potential to give them a good start in life.

This resource has been specifically tailored to prepare students for sitting apprenticeship or VET/TAFE admission tests, and for giving students the basic skills they will need for a career in trade. In many ways, it is a win-win situation, with students enjoying and studying relevant maths for trades and Registered Training Organisations (RTOs) receiving students that have improved basic maths and literacy skills.

All that is needed is patience, hard work, a positive attitude, a belief in yourself that you can do it and a desire to achieve. The rest is up to you.

About the author

Andrew Spencer has studied education both within Australia and overseas. He has a Bachelor of Education, as well as a Masters of Science in which he specialised in teacher education. Andrew has extensive experience in teaching secondary mathematics throughout New South Wales and South Australia for well over fifteen years. He has taught a range of subject areas including Maths, English, Science, Classics, Physical Education and Technical Studies. His sense of the importance of practical mathematics continued to develop with the range of subject areas he taught in.

Acknowledgements

For Paula, Zach, Katelyn, Mum and Dad.
    Many thanks to Mal Aubrey (GTA) and all training organisations for their input.
    To the De La Salle Brothers for their selfless work with all students.
    Thanks also to Dr. Pauline Carter for her unwavering support for all maths teachers.
    This is for all students who value learning, who are willing to work hard and who have character …
and are characters!

Unit 1: Spelling

Short-answer questions

Specific instructions to students

- This is an exercise to help you to identify and correct spelling errors.
- Read the activity below, then answer accordingly.

Read the following passage and identify and correct the spelling errors:

> A sallon opens at 9.00 a.m. on a Saterday morning. The staff arive at 8.00 a.m. to begin proparing for a bussy day, as severel curstomers are getting maried and they are arriving soon to have their hair designed. The managor imediately gets the staff to ready the equipment as the first custamer is due in 45 minates. The scisors need stearalising again as the aprentice dropped them on the floor only minutes before. In adision, the floor had not been swapt from the previours day as it was a publik holiday and everyone was grateful for the day off. At 9.00 a.m. the first customer appers at the salon's doors.

Incorrect words:

_____

_____

Correct words:

_____

_____

Unit 2: Alphabetising

Short-answer questions

Specific instructions to students

- In this unit, you will be able to practise your alphabetising skills.
- Read the activity below, then answer accordingly.

Put the following words into alphabetical order:

skeleton brush	colour
barber chair	tint
sterilise	trimmer
brush	hair gel
tail comb	bob cut
hair oil	fringe
mousse	conditioner

Short-answer questions

Specific instructions to students

- This is an exercise to help you understand what you read.
- Read the following activity, then answer the questions that follow.

Read the following passage and answer the questions in sentence form.

Jill, the salon owner, had a busy Friday to deal with. She arrived at 7.45 a.m. and she knew the day would be hectic. One stylist had called in sick and there were five brides booked in to have their hair done. As Philip, the new apprentice, arrived Jill got him into work straight away. One customer required a perm, while there were three other customers who needed their hair washed and prepared for cutting. A few women were booked in for tinting, which was going to keep Philip busy for some time as he needed to prepare the tint. Philip found that all of the customers were patient and he provided them with tea and coffee as they waited. Another apprentice, Elle, started dismantling the trimmer and cleaning the whole unit. Christine, one of the staff, started cutting a customer's hair as one of the work experience students assisted by sweeping around the chair. The day continued to get busier after that. By the time Jill and the rest of her staff had clocked out at 6.00 p.m., she was looking forward to heading out to meet with friends for drinks.

QUESTION 1
Why did Jill think that the day was going to be a busy one?

Answer:

QUESTION 2
What was the first job that Jill got Philip started on?

Answer:

QUESTION 3
What was the task that was going to keep Philip busy?

Answer:

QUESTION 4
What job did the work experience student have to do?

Answer:

QUESTION 5
How long was Jill's work day, from when she arrived at the salon until the time that she left?

Answer:

MATHEMATICS

Unit 4: General Mathematics

Short-answer questions

Specific instructions to students

- This unit will help you to improve your general mathematical skills.
- Read the following questions and answer all of them in the spaces provided.
- You may not use a calculator.
- You need to show all working.

QUESTION 1

What unit of measurement would you use to measure:

a   the length of hair extensions?

Answer:

_____

b   the temperature of steriliser?

Answer:

_____

c   the amount of hair conditioner?

Answer:

_____

d   the weight of a barber's chair?

Answer:

_____

e   the voltage of a hair dryer?

Answer:

_____

f   the length of a tail comb?

Answer:

_____

g   the cost of a trim?

Answer:

_____

QUESTION 2

Write an example of the following and give an instance where it may be found in the hairdressing industry:

a   percentages

Answer:

_____

b   decimals

Answer:

_____

c fractions

Answer:

d mixed numbers

Answer:

e ratios

Answer:

f angles

Answer:

QUESTION 3
Convert the following units:

a 12 kg to grams

Answer:

b 4 t to kilograms

Answer:

c 120 cm to metres

Answer:

d 1140 mL to litres

Answer:

e 1650 g to kilograms

Answer:

f 1880 kg to tonnes

Answer:

g 13 m to centimetres

Answer:

h 4.5 L to millilitres

Answer:

QUESTION 4
Write the following in descending order:

0.4   0.04   4.1   40.0   400.00   4.0

Answer:

QUESTION 5
Write the decimal number that is between the following:

a 0.2 and 0.4

Answer:

b 1.8 and 1.9

Answer:

c 12.4 and 12.5

Answer:

d 28.3 and 28.4

Answer:

e 101.5 and 101.7

Answer:

QUESTION 6
Round off the following numbers to two decimal places:

a 12.346

Answer:

9780170462839

b   2.251

Answer:

___

c   123.897

Answer:

___

d   688.882

Answer:

___

e   1209.741

Answer:

___

QUESTION 7
Estimate the following by approximation:

a   1288 × 19 =

Answer:

___

b   201 × 20 =

Answer:

___

c   497 × 12.2 =

Answer:

___

d   1008 × 10.3 =

Answer:

___

e   399 × 22 =

Answer:

___

f   201 − 19 =

Answer:

___

g   502 − 61 =

Answer:

___

h   1003 − 49 =

Answer:

___

i   10 001 − 199 =

Answer:

___

j   99.99 − 39.8 =

Answer:

___

QUESTION 8
What do the following add up to?

a $4, $4.99 and $144.95

Answer:

___

b   8.75, 6.9 and 12.55

Answer:

___

c   65 mL, 18 mL and 209 mL

Answer:

___

d   21.3 g, 119 g and 884.65 g

Answer:

___

QUESTION 9
Subtract the following:

a   2338 from 7117

Answer:

___

b 1786 from 3112

Answer:

_____

c 5979 from 8014

Answer:

_____

d 11 989 from 26 221

Answer:

_____

e 108 767 from 231 111

Answer:

_____

QUESTION 10

Use division to solve the following:

a $2177 \div 7 =$

Answer:

_____

b $4484 \div 4 =$

Answer:

_____

c $63.9 \div 0.3 =$

Answer:

_____

d $121.63 \div 1.2 =$

Answer:

_____

e $466.88 \div 0.8 =$

Answer:

_____

The following information is provided for Question 11.

To solve using BODMAS, in order from left to right, solve the Brackets first, then Of, then Division, then Multiplication, then Addition and lastly Subtraction. The following example has been done for your reference.

EXAMPLE :

Solve $(4 \times 7) \times 2 + 6 - 4$.

STEP 1

Solve the Brackets first: $(4 \times 7) = 28$

STEP 2

No Division so next solve Multiplication: $28 \times 2 = 56$

STEP 3

Addition is next: $56 + 6 = 62$

STEP 4

Subtraction is the last process: $62 - 4 = 58$

FINAL ANSWER

58

QUESTION 11

Using BODMAS, solve:

a $(6 \times 9) \times 5 + 7 - 2 =$

Answer:

_____

b $(9 \times 8) \times 4 + 6 - 1 =$

Answer:

_____

c $3 \times (5 \times 7) + 11 - 8 =$

Answer:

_____

d $5 \times (8 \times 3) + 9 - 6 =$

Answer:

_____

e $7 + 6 \times 3 + (9 \times 6) - 9 =$

Answer:

_____

f $6 + 9 \times 4 + (6 \times 7) - 21 =$

Answer:

_____

9780170462839

Unit 5: Basic Operations

Section A: Addition

QUESTION 1

An apprentice purchases items for the salon which includes: a styling chair for $225, barber scissors for $65 and a washing basin for $385. What would be the total cost?

Answer:

_____

QUESTION 2

A student had a haircut costing $29; another customer had a tint costing $50; another had a half-head of foils costing $120. What is the total cost?

Answer:

_____

QUESTION 3

A hair salon wholesaler stocks 127 gowns, 268 jars of hair mousse and 323 various pairs of disposable gloves. How many items are in stock, in total?

Answer:

_____

QUESTION 4

A hairdresser completes cuts at the following prices: a style cut for $21, a senior's cut for $16, a university student's cut for $19, a high school student's cut for $17 and a primary school student's cut for $10. How much is the total cost for the cuts?

Answer:

_____

QUESTION 5

A hairdresser uses the following amounts of hair gel in May: 355 mL in week one, 429 mL in week two, 869 mL in week three and 662 mL in week four.

a   How many millilitres have been used?

Answer:

_____

b   How many litres have been used?

Answer:

_____

QUESTION 6

An apprentice hairdresser buys a hair care water-mist trigger spray bottle for $8.00, a black cutting cape for $12.00, a hair scissors pouch holster for $19.00 and a ceramic hair straightener for $65.00. How much has been spent?

Answer:

_____

QUESTION 7

A salon stocks a pack of 300 pre-cut and folded hair foils for $13, 50 salon human-hair black extension clips for $12 and 30 mL of salon hair treatment for $15. What is the total cost of the items?

Answer:

_____

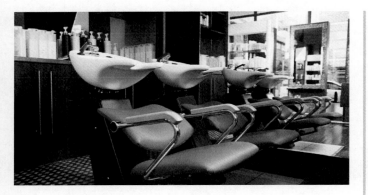

QUESTION 8

An apprentice buys the following stock for the salon: a square booster seat for $55, a hydraulic styling chair for $245 and a shampoo basin for $650. How much has been spent?

Answer:

QUESTION 9

A hairdresser working in the country travels 36 km, 98 km, 77 km and 104 km to cut the hair of four different elderly customers. How far has been travelled?

Answer:

QUESTION 10

Three separate hair styles cost $78, $88 and $93. How much does the total come to?

Answer:

Section B: Subtraction

Short-answer questions

Specific instructions to students

- This section will help you to improve your subtraction skills for basic operations.
- Read the following questions and answer all of them in the spaces provided.
- You may not use a calculator.
- You need to show all working.

QUESTION 1

A customer comes to a salon with hair that is 52 cm in length. The hairdresser trims off 22 cm but the customer is not satisfied and wants shorter hair. If a further 7 cm is cut off, what length remains?

Answer:

QUESTION 2

If one hairdresser travels 36 km to and from work and another hairdresser travels 19 km, how much further has the first hairdresser travelled than the second?

Answer:

QUESTION 3

Apprentice A completes style cuts and charges $243. Apprentice B also completes style cuts and charges $147. How much more has Apprentice A charged?

Answer:

QUESTION 4

A hairdresser uses 39 hair clips from a box that has contained 163 hair clips over a month. How many are left?

Answer:

QUESTION 5

A perm costs $144.50. The manager takes off a discount of $15.00. How much does the customer need to pay?

Answer:

QUESTION 6

Over the course of a year, an apprentice uses 316 hair extensions from a box containing 500 hair extensions. How many are left in the box?

Answer:

9780170462839

QUESTION 7

A salon uses the following amounts of hair conditioner for three cuts: Cut A = 55 mL; Cut B = 38 mL and Cut C = 69 mL. How much conditioner is left from a bottle that contained 250 mL of conditioner to begin with?

Answer:

QUESTION 8

A salon manager records 74 cuts in one week. If there were a total of 93 cuts booked, how many customers did not turn up or cancelled?

Answer:

QUESTION 9

The overall takings for a salon, for a year, were $171 113. The cost of staff wages came to $84 239. How much was left?

Answer:

QUESTION 10

A hairdresser uses the following amounts of the same tint on three separate styles: 80 mL, 60 mL and 50 mL. If there were 250 mL of tint in a tube to begin with, how much would be left?

Answer:

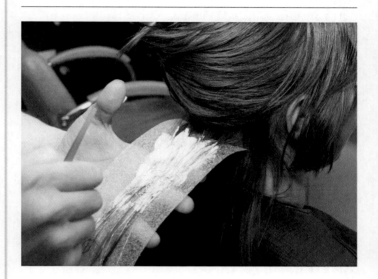

Section C: Multiplication

Short-answer questions

Specific instructions to students

- This section will help you to improve your multiplication skills for basic operations.
- Read the following questions and answer all of them in the spaces provided.
- You may not use a calculator.
- You need to show all working.

QUESTION 1

If a standard cut costs $25, how much would nine similar standard cuts cost?

Answer:

QUESTION 2

If a perm costs $80, how much would three perms total?

Answer:

QUESTION 3

An apprentice uses 35 mL of permanent hair colour on one specific style. How much hair colour is used for the same style, if it is completed six times in one month?

Answer:

QUESTION 4

A salon purchases six new hydraulic styling chairs at a cost of $239 each. What would the total cost be?

Answer:

QUESTION 5

A salon purchases three new shampoo basins at a cost of $625 each. How much would the total cost be?

Answer:

QUESTION 6

A hairdresser charges $115 for a regrowth plus colour-balance-on-ends treatment. How much is charged for eight of the same treatments?

Answer:

QUESTION 7

A salon uses 9 litres of gel every month. How much gel is used over 18 months?

Answer:

QUESTION 8

If a salon uses 27 pairs of disposable gloves per week, how many would be used over a month (four weeks)?

Answer:

QUESTION 9

If a hairdresser uses three towels each hour, how many would be used over an eight-hour day?

Answer:

QUESTION 10

If a customer who lives in the country travels at 110 km/h for five hours to attend a salon, how far have they travelled in total?

Answer:

Section D: Division

Short-answer questions

Specific instructions to students

- This section will help you to improve your division skills for basic operations.
- Read the following questions and answer all of them in the spaces provided.
- You may not use a calculator.
- You need to show all working.

QUESTION 1

A salon has 24 customers booked in on a Friday morning. If there are four chairs and four hairdressers working, how many customers will each hairdresser attend?

Answer:

QUESTION 2

If a hairdresser earns $868 (before tax) for working a five-day week, how much would they earn per day?

Answer:

9780170462839

QUESTION 3

A salon owner buys 210 bottles of anti-dandruff shampoo in bulk. Each box contains 30 bottles. How many boxes are there?

Answer:

_____

QUESTION 4

A hairdresser has 720 customers in six months. On average, how many customers are there per month?

Answer:

_____

QUESTION 5

An apprentice puts streaks in four customers' hair. The total cost comes to $260. How much is this per customer, on average?

Answer:

_____

QUESTION 6

One month's takings for a salon are $13 925. How much are the takings, on average, per week (given that there four weeks in each month)?

Answer:

_____

QUESTION 7

At a yearly stocktake, a store person at a hairdressing wholesaler warehouse counts 648 scissors. If they are packed so that there are six in each box, how many boxes would there be?

Answer:

_____

QUESTION 8

Four hundred and eight gowns are ordered for a salon. If there are four in each packet, how many packets are there?

Answer:

_____

QUESTION 9

A salon has takings of $6862 over six days. How much, on average, does the salon make per day?

Answer:

_____

QUESTION 10

An apprentice uses 144 foils on 12 customers. How many foils is this per customer, on average?

Answer:

_____

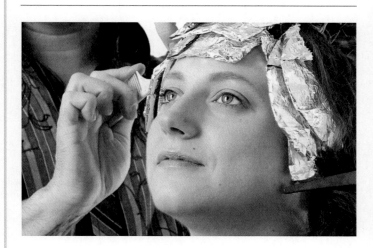

Unit 6: Decimals

Section A: Addition

Short-answer questions

Specific instructions to students

- This section will help you to improve your addition skills when working with decimals.
- Read the following questions and answer all of them in the spaces provided.
- You may not use a calculator.
- You need to show all working.

QUESTION 1

If four new lockable hairdressing trolleys are purchased for $946.88 and a hairdresser chair for $209.75, how much is the total?

Answer:

QUESTION 2

An apprentice hairdresser buys a set of brushes for $39.95, some hair bleach for $24.95, several combs for $44.55 and a set of curlers for $59.45. How much has been spent?

Answer:

QUESTION 3

The length of one hair extension is 25.5 cm and another is 30.5 cm. What is the total length of the two extensions?

Answer:

QUESTION 4

A customer purchases a tint brush for $15.50 and a round brush for $8.50. How much is the total?

Answer:

QUESTION 5

A hairdresser buys the following: a magazine on hairstyling for $8.99, hair clips for $6.50, hair oil for $12.30 and an apron for $5.90. What is the total?

Answer:

QUESTION 6

If a truck driver who delivers salon products travels 65.8 km, 36.5 km, 22.7 km and 89.9 km, how far has the driver travelled to deliver the goods?

Answer:

QUESTION 7

A customer asks for a single foil that costs $7.50 and his partner wants three foils costing $22.50. What is the total?

Answer:

QUESTION 8

Two customers ask for three foils costing $22.50 and nine foils costing $67.50 respectively. How much will the total cost be for each customer?

Answer:

QUESTION 9

A hair stylist completes three cuts. The first cut is $45.80, the second is $130.65 and the third is $66.45. How much has been charged in total?

Answer:

QUESTION 10

A salon's takings for the first hour after opening are $89.90, $45.50, $55.50, $135.50 and $32.50. What are the total takings for the first hour?

Answer:

Section B: Subtraction

QUESTION 1

A salon's takings in the morning are $338.68. The manager pays for lunch for the staff and spends $43.95 on food and drinks. How much is left in the float?

Answer:

QUESTION 2

A fourth year apprentice gets paid $768.50 for a week's work. If $118.55 is used to pay bills, $55.75 is paid for petrol and $76 is spent on entertainment, how much is left?

Answer:

QUESTION 3

A hairdresser completes a style that costs $189.50 and then a discount of $25.00 is given. How much is the final cost?

Answer:

QUESTION 4

A first year apprentice works 38 hours and earns $245.60. The apprentice uses $48.85 for petrol and $38.75 for going out. How much is left?

Answer:

QUESTION 5

A customer wants one-quarter-head foils that cost $90.50. The customer pays with 2 × $50 notes. How much change is given?

Answer:

QUESTION 6

If a customer pays $22.50 for a haircut with 2 × $20 notes, how much change is given?

Answer:

QUESTION 7

The members of a bridal party have their hair styled for the wedding day. The total comes to $432.50. What change is given if five $100 notes are used to pay the bill?

Answer:

QUESTON 8

A 250 mL tube of hair colour is used on three different hairstyles: 25 mL for the first style, 36 mL on the second and 13 mL on the third. How much is left in the tube?

Answer:

QUESTION 9

A hairdresser buys two hairdryers for $326.50. If 8 × $50 notes are used to pay the bill, how much change is given?

Answer:

QUESTION 10

A salon has four customers that require different treatments. One customer has shrink-cap streaks ($68.50); another customer has half-head foils, including tonal deposit ($99.50); another customer has a dimensional lift and support ($69.50); and the fourth customer has a solid global colour ($72.00). If the salon float has $1186 in it after the customers have paid for the treatments, how much was in the float before they paid?

Answer:

Section C: Multiplication

QUESTION 1

If one tint brush costs $9.95, how much will five tint brushes cost?

Answer:

QUESTION 2

If an apprentice uses six jars of hair gel on average each week, how many jars are used in one year?

Answer:

QUESTION 3

A salon manager replaces six pairs of six-inch scissors at a cost of $34.50 each. What is the total?

Answer:

QUESTION 4

If a salon purchases six model bald heads that cost $38.65 per head, how much is the total cost?

Answer:

QUESTION 5

A manager buys 12 capes that cost $19.95 each. What is the total cost?

Answer:

QUESTION 6

An apprentice earns $15.50 per hour. If the working week totals 45 hours, how much is earned in a week?

Answer:

QUESTION 7

The manager of a hairdressing franchise buys air conditioners at $682.50 per unit for her eight salons. How much has been spent?

Answer:

QUESTION 8

A salon product delivery van drops off 75 one-litre conditioner bottles to a salon at a cost of $19.85 per bottle. How much will the invoice total be?

Answer:

QUESTION 9

A manager purchases five gallery workstations for the salon at a cost of $255 each. How much is the outlay?

Answer:

QUESTION 10

A hairdresser earns $130.65 per day before tax. How much is earned for a five-day week?

Answer:

Section D: Division

QUESTION 1

A hairdresser earns $628.55 for a six-day working week. How much is earned for each day?

Answer:

_____

QUESTION 2

A manager earns $790.60 for five days work. How much is earned per day?

Answer:

_____

QUESTION 3

A salon's takings are $2245.50 over five days. How much are the daily takings, on average?

Answer:

_____

QUESTION 4

A stylist completes root re-touches on three customers. The total cost comes to $312.90. How much is this, on average, per customer?

Answer:

_____

QUESTION 5

Three customers have full-head foils at a total cost of $450.90. How much is each customer charged?

Answer:

_____

QUESTION 6

Four customers have long hair that requires a wash, cut and blow-dry. The total bill comes to $180.80. How much does each customer pay?

Answer:

_____

QUESTION 7

Six female customers are charged the same amount to have a shampoo, style cut and blow-dry. The takings come to $453.00. How much is each customer charged?

Answer:

_____

QUESTION 8

A salon completes five permanent colour regrowth applications for five different customers. The total charged for all five applications is $427.50. How much is each customer charged?

Answer:

_____

QUESTION 9

Eight customers are charged a total of $364.80 to get highlights using the balayage technique. How much is the cost per customer?

Answer:

_____

QUESTION 10

Three customers with short hair have a colour gloss treatment. The total comes to $226.50. How much is each customer charged?

Answer:

_____

Unit 7: Fractions

Section A: Addition

Short-answer questions

Specific instructions to students

- This section is designed to help you to improve your addition skills when working with fractions.
- Read the following questions and answer all of them in the spaces provided.
- You may not use a calculator.
- You need to show all working.

QUESTION 1

$\frac{1}{2} + \frac{4}{5} =$

Answer:

QUESTION 2

$2\frac{2}{4} + 1\frac{2}{3} =$

Answer:

QUESTION 3

Two bottles of shampoo are each $\frac{1}{3}$ full. How much shampoo, as a fraction of a bottle, is there in total?

Answer:

QUESTION 4

An apprentice has two customers who want foils. One customer wants one-quarter-head foils and the other customer wants three-quarter-head foils. Using a fraction, show the total amount of head foils.

Answer:

QUESTION 5

A tint bowl has $\frac{2}{3}$ of a small bottle of red hair colour in it. To make a shade of orange, another $\frac{1}{4}$ of a small bottle of yellow hair colour is added. How much hair colour in total is in the tint bowl, as a fraction?

Answer:

Section B: Subtraction

Short-answer questions

Specific instructions to students

- This section is designed to help you to improve your subtraction skills when working with fractions.
- Read the following questions and answer all of them in the spaces provided.
- You may not use a calculator.
- You need to show all working.

QUESTION 1

$\frac{2}{3} - \frac{1}{4} =$

Answer:

QUESTION 2

$2\frac{2}{3} - 1\frac{1}{4} =$

Answer:

9780170462839

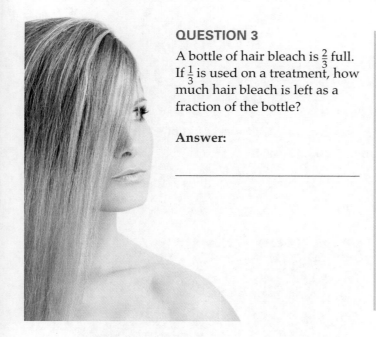

QUESTION 3

A bottle of hair bleach is $\frac{2}{3}$ full. If $\frac{1}{3}$ is used on a treatment, how much hair bleach is left as a fraction of the bottle?

Answer:

_____

QUESTION 4

A hairdresser has $2\frac{1}{2}$ containers of hair gel. If $1\frac{1}{3}$ is used on two different customers, how much hair gel is left, as a fraction of a container?

Answer:

_____

QUESTION 5

An apprentice has $2\frac{3}{4}$ bottles of permanent hair colour in a salon. If $1\frac{1}{2}$ bottles are used over two weeks, how much is left in total as a fraction?

Answer:

_____

Section C: Multiplication

Short-answer questions

Specific instructions to students

- This section is designed to help you to improve your multiplication skills when working with fractions.
- Read the following questions and answer all of them in the spaces provided.
- You may not use a calculator.
- You need to show all working.

QUESTION 1

$\frac{2}{4} \times \frac{2}{3} =$

Answer:

_____

QUESTION 2

$2\frac{2}{3} \times 1\frac{1}{2} =$

Answer:

_____

QUESTION 3

An apprentice uses two bottles of conditioner that are each $\frac{2}{3}$ full. What is the total amount of conditioner used as a fraction?

Answer:

_____

QUESTION 4

A hairdresser uses three bottles of hair bleach that are $\frac{3}{4}$ full over a week. How much is used as a fraction?

Answer:

_____

QUESTION 5

A hairdresser uses four small bottles of hair colour that are each $\frac{1}{3}$ full over a week. How much is used as a fraction?

Answer:

_____

Section D: Division

QUESTION 1

$\frac{2}{3} \div \frac{1}{4} =$

Answer:

QUESTION 2

$2\frac{3}{4} \div 1\frac{1}{3} =$

Answer:

QUESTION 3

An apprentice needs to distribute the contents of three bleach bottles evenly into four empty bottles in order to dilute the bleach. As a fraction, how much will be in each of the four bottles?

Answer:

QUESTION 4

A hairdresser has three empty bottles and two full bottles of hair colour. He wants to transfer and then mix the colour. He needs to transfer the hair colour evenly to each empty bottle. As a fraction, how much colour will be evenly transferred to each of the three empty bottles?

Answer:

QUESTION 5

A hairdresser wants to apply a tint and needs the colour diluted. Two bottles of colour are poured into six empty bottles. As a fraction, how much will be poured into each of the six empty bottles from the two full colour bottles?

Answer:

Unit 8: Percentages

Short-answer questions

Specific instructions to students

- In this unit, you will be able to practise and improve your skills in working out percentages.
- Read the following questions and answer all of them in the spaces provided.
- You may not use a calculator.
- You need to show all working.

10% rule: Move the decimal one place to the left to get 10%.

EXAMPLE

10% of $45.00 would be $4.50

QUESTION 1

A bill for style cuts for two bridesmaids comes to $220.00. The customer has a voucher for a 10% discount.

a   What will the discount be?

Answer:

_____

b   What will the bill come to after the 10% is taken off?

Answer:

_____

QUESTION 2

A customer has full-head foils costing $175.00. A '10% off' voucher is used to reduce the final cost.

a   How much will the discount be?

Answer:

_____

b   How much is the final bill?

Answer:

_____

QUESTION 3

A salon purchases an air conditioner for $1198.50. The salon was given a 10% discount on the purchase.

a   How much will the discount be?

Answer:

_____

b   What is the final cost?

Answer:

_____

QUESTION 4

A manager buys five lady shavers at a wholesale price of $124.80. A 5% discount is given.

a   How much is the discount worth?

Answer:

_____

b   What is the final total? (Hint: Find 10%, halve it, then subtract it from the individual price of each shaver.)

Answer:

_____

QUESTION 5

An apprentice buys three gowns for $20 each, a hair dryer for $69 and a set of hair rollers for $13.

a   How much is the total?

Answer:

_____

b   How much would be a 20% discount?

Answer:

_____

c   What is the final cost after discount?

Answer:

_____

QUESTION 6

The following items are purchased for a salon: one box of disposable gloves costing $18, 12 bottles of sculpting mousse for $109, a professional clipper for $19.99, a hair dryer for $72 and six towels for $49.

a   What is the total?

Answer:

_____

b   How much would be a 10% discount?

Answer:

_____

c   What is the final cost after the discount?

Answer:

_____

QUESTION 7

A salon offers 20% off the price of any store product as long as the customer spends at least $100. If a customer spends $105, how much would a set of round brushes, normally priced at $36, cost?

Answer:

_____

QUESTION 8

A particular range of hair care products are discounted by 15%. If the recommended retail price is $45.50 for one of these particular products, what will be the discounted price?

Answer:

_____

QUESTION 9

A brand of hair spray costs $16.90 as per the recommended retail price. The store has a '20% sale' on this item. How much will the hair spray cost during the sale?

Answer:

_____

QUESTION 10

Shampoo and conditioner for damaged hair retails for $29. During a sale, the product is sold at 30% off. What will the selling price be after the discount?

Answer:

_____

9780170462839

Unit 9: Measurement Conversions

Short-answer questions

Specific instructions to students

- This unit is designed to help you to improve your skills and increase your speed in converting one measurement into another.
- Read the following questions and answer all of them in the spaces provided.
- You may not use a calculator.
- You need to show all working.

QUESTION 1
How many millimetres are there in 1 cm?

Answer:

_____

QUESTION 2
How many centimetres are there in 1 m?

Answer:

_____

QUESTION 3
How many millimetres are there in 1 m?

Answer:

_____

QUESTION 4
If there are two braids in 2 cm, how many braids would be in 10 cm?

Answer:

_____

QUESTION 5
How many millilitres are there in a 1.5 L bottle of anti-dandruff shampoo?

Answer:

_____

QUESTION 6
How many litres does 3500 mL of hair bleach make?

Answer:

_____

QUESTION 7
A barber's chair weighs a quarter of a tonne. How many kilograms is that?

Answer:

_____

QUESTION 8
A delivery truck weighs 2 t. How many kilograms is that?

Answer:

_____

QUESTION 9
A hair product delivery truck weighs 4750 kg. How many tonnes is that?

Answer:

_____

QUESTION 10
A salon floor measures 4.8 m wide and 12 m long. How far is it around the perimeter of the salon?

Answer:

_____

From time to time, it will be important to be able to convert inches to centimetres, especially when selecting lengths for hair extensions.

Remember: 1 inch = 2.54 cm (you can round this down to 2.5 cm if you wish)

QUESTION 11
Julie is a first year apprentice who is asked to use hair extensions that are 5 inches. What would this length be in centimetres?

Answer:

_____

QUESTION 12

On Tuesday, Pauline had two customers who wanted hair extensions. One customer wanted 8-inch hair extensions and the other wanted 12-inch hair extensions. What lengths are these in centimetres?

Answer:

QUESTION 13

Jake is going to the end of year formal and he wants 18-inch hair extensions. How long will these be in centimetres?

Answer:

QUESTION 14

Rachel was working on a mannequin and wanted to add 14-inch human hair extensions. How long would they be in centimetres?

Answer:

QUESTION 15

Paula loved long hair and decided to get 20-inch hair extensions. How long would her hair extensions be in centimetres?

Answer:

QUESTION 16

Lakkari wanted 25 cm hair extensions. How long would these be in inches? (Hint: divide 25 by 2.5)

Answer:

QUESTION 17

A mannequin hair model has hair added at a length of 30 cm. How long is this in inches?

Answer:

QUESTION 18

Kalyan is getting married on Saturday. She wants to have hair extensions that are 50 cm long. How long will the hair extensions be in inches?

Answer:

QUESTION 19

Gabrielle enters a salon and wants a short haircut. The cut is to be 5 cm long. What length is this in inches?

Answer:

QUESTION 20

After washing a customer's long hair, Daryle asks that it be trimmed to a length of approximately 35 cm. How long is this in inches?

Answer:

9780170462839

Unit 10: Earning Wages

- This unit will help you to calculate how much a job is worth and how long you need to complete the job.
- Read the following questions and answer all of them in the spaces provided.
- You may not use a calculator.
- You need to show all working.

QUESTION 1

Sue, the first year apprentice, earns $260.60 net (take home per week). How much does Sue earn per year? (Remember, there are 52 weeks in a year.)

Answer:

QUESTION 2

A hairdresser starts work at 8.00 a.m. and has a break at 10.30 a.m. for 20 minutes. Lunch starts at 12.30 p.m. and finishes at 1.30 p.m. The hairdresser then works through to 4.00 p.m.

a How long are the breaks in total, in minutes?

Answer:

b How many hours and minutes have been worked in total, excluding breaks?

Answer:

QUESTION 3

A hairdresser earns $12.50 an hour and works a 38-hour week. How much are his weekly gross earnings (before tax)?

Answer:

QUESTION 4

A hairdresser gets paid $513 net for her week's work. From her earnings she buys new clothes at a cost of $46.90, jewellery worth $49.50, CDs worth $59.97 and a bus ticket which costs $12.60. She also spends $55 on entertainment.

a What is the total of all money spent?

Answer:

b How much is left?

Answer:

QUESTION 5

Several customers enter a salon and the hairdresser there takes the following amount of time for each customer: 34 minutes, 18 minutes, 7 minutes, 44 minutes and 59 minutes. How much time, in minutes and hours, has been spent on these customers in total?

Answer:

QUESTION 6

A hairdresser has a customer who requires permanent hair colouring. This takes the hairdresser $1\frac{1}{2}$ hours to complete. How many hours are left if the hairdresser normally works an 8-hour day?

Answer:

QUESTION 7

A hairdresser wants to create more movement and greater lift in a hair style for a customer. This takes $1\frac{1}{2}$ hours to complete. A second customer requires a regrowth treatment plus colour balance on the ends. This takes $1\frac{1}{4}$ hours.

a   How many hours were spent on the two customers? State your answer as a fraction.

Answer:

_____

b   If the hairdresser works an 8-hour day, how many hours are left? State your answer as a fraction.

Answer:

_____

QUESTION 8

A salon charges $230 for a permanent wave treatment for long hair. If this takes the hairdresser 1 hour and 45 minutes to complete, how long (in hours and minutes) will be left in an 8-hour working day?

Answer:

_____

QUESTION 9

A salon manager begins work at 7.00 a.m. and works until 4.00 p.m. She takes a morning break for 20 minutes, a lunch break for 60 minutes and an afternoon break of 20 minutes.

a   How much time has been spent on breaks?

Answer:

_____

b   How much time has been spent working?

Answer:

_____

QUESTION 10

A salon's daily takings come to $850.50. If the salon manager spent 10 hours at the salon working alone, how much is the rate, on average, of the takings per hour?

Answer:

_____

9780170462839

Unit 11: Squaring Numbers

Section A: Introducing square numbers

Short-answer questions

Specific instructions to students

- This section is designed to help you to improve your skills and increase your speed in squaring numbers.
- Read the following questions and answer all of them in the spaces provided.
- You may not use a calculator.
- You need to show all working.

Any number squared is multiplied by itself.

EXAMPLE

4 squared $= 4^2 = 4 \times 4 = 16$

QUESTION 1

$6^2 =$

Answer:

QUESTION 2

$8^2 =$

Answer:

QUESTION 3

$12^2 =$

Answer:

QUESTION 4

$3^2 =$

Answer:

QUESTION 5

$7^2 =$

Answer:

QUESTION 6

$11^2 =$

Answer:

QUESTION 7

$10^2 =$

Answer:

QUESTION 8

$9^2 =$

Answer:

QUESTION 9

$2^2 =$

Answer:

QUESTION 10

$4^2 =$

Answer:

Section B: Applying square numbers to the trade

QUESTION 1

If there are 5 × 5 hair spray cans in a box, how many cans are there in total?

Answer:

QUESTION 2

A box of shampoo arrives at a salon stacked 6 × 6. What is the total number of bottles of shampoo?

Answer:

QUESTION 3

There are 12 × 12 round brushes packed into a box. How many are in the box?

Answer:

QUESTION 4

A warehouse floor has an area that is 15 m × 15 m. How much floor area is this in square metres (m²)?

Answer:

QUESTION 5

A merchandise box contains hair gel tubes that are in rows of 8 × 8. How many tubes of hair gel are there?

Answer:

QUESTION 6

A salon manager unpacks two boxes to put on display. The first box contains 4 × 4 cans of hair spray. The second box contains mannequin heads that are packed in a 3 × 3 formation. How many stock items are there in total?

Answer:

QUESTION 7

A box of shampoo and conditioner bottles arrive at a salon. If they are packed in a 20 × 20 formation, how many are there?

Answer:

QUESTION 8

A salon stocks the following: 5 × 5 tint bowls, 3 × 3 capes and 7 × 7 skeleton brushes. How many items of stock are there in total?

Answer:

QUESTION 9

A strand set consists of 5 × 5-inch light strands, 5 × 5-inch medium strands and 5 × 5-inch dark strands. How many individual strands are there in total?

Answer:

QUESTION 10

A hair swatch kit consists of the following: 3 × 3 dark pieces; 3 × 3 medium pieces; 3 × 3 medium-dark pieces and 3 × 3 white pieces. How many pieces are there in total?

Answer:

Unit 12: Vouchers

QUESTION 1

A customer has a wash, cut and blow-dry that comes to $50. The customer has a voucher for 20% off.

a How much is taken off for the voucher?

Answer:

b How much is the final cost?

Answer:

QUESTION 2

A father and his son get their hair washed, cut and blow-dried before returning to work and school respectively after the holidays. The salon charges $45 for the father's cut and $25 for the son's haircut. They also purchase hair gel for $8.50, shampoo for $13.50 and a new skeleton brush for $12.50. They have a '15% off' voucher that covers both cuts and products.

a What is the total before taking off the value of the voucher?

Answer:

b How much is the voucher worth?

Answer:

c What is the total after the value of the voucher is taken off?

Answer:

QUESTION 3

A customer purchases some goods from a salon. They include: two jars of hair gel for $22.95, a skeleton brush for $15.95, a fine tail comb for $9.99 and texturiser with a handle for $14.95. The customer has a '30% off' voucher on all items.

a What is the total cost before using the voucher?

Answer:

b How much is the voucher worth?

Answer:

c What is the final cost after using the voucher?

Answer:

QUESTION 4

A family of four comes into a salon for haircuts. One person has their roots re-touched, which costs $95; another person has a tint costing $50; a child has a haircut costing $15 and another child has short hair that requires a treatment costing $45. The family has a voucher for '25% off'.

a What is the total before using the voucher?

Answer:

b How much is the voucher worth?

Answer:

c What will be the final total after using the voucher?

Answer:

QUESTION 5

A salon manager purchases equipment to update their salon. The manager buys four hairdresser chairs for $968, two lockable hairdressing trolleys for $525, six dozen bleach-proof towels for $348 and three mannequin heads for $65. The manager has a '15% off' voucher on all goods.

a   What is the total before using the voucher?

Answer:

_____

b   How much is the voucher worth?

Answer:

_____

c   How much will the salon manager need to pay after using the voucher?

Answer:

_____

QUESTION 6

A customer enters a salon with a '25% off' gift voucher that she received for her birthday. The customer decides to have foils so as to have streaks of colour to help give her hair definition. The cost is $155.00.

a   How much will the voucher take off the cost?

Answer:

_____

b   What will the final cost be?

Answer:

_____

QUESTION 7

Three customers in a salon have vouchers for '15% off'. They have style cuts that cost $60, $35 and $25. The costs include individual design for each customer's hair, expert cutting, shampooing, conditioning and blow-waving.

a   How much does the voucher reduce the cost for each customer?

Answer:

_____

b   How much is the total for each customer after using the voucher?

Answer:

_____

_____

QUESTION 8

A wedding party is booked in for style cuts on the morning of the wedding. The bride's cut costs $110. There are four bridesmaids and each cut costs $95. The bridal party has a '15% off' gift voucher as a present from some of the guests.

a   What is the cost before the voucher?

Answer:

_____

b   By how much will the voucher reduce the price?

Answer:

_____

c   What is the final cost to the bridal party?

Answer:

_____

QUESTION 9

A local salon approaches a high school and offers '15% off' vouchers to students wanting to have their haircut for the upcoming Year 11 formal. Eighty-three students decide to take up the offer. The cost of each cut before using the voucher is $55.00.

a   What is the total cost for all 83 students to get their haircut before using the voucher?

Answer:

_____

b   What is the cost for one cut after using the '15% off' voucher?

Answer:

_____

9780170462839

c How much in total will the '15% off' vouchers take off the price for the whole group of 83 students?

Answer:

---

d What will the final takings be for the salon from the group of 83 students?

Answer:

QUESTION 10

The Year 12 formal is in a week and a salon decides to offer vouchers to any students who want to get their haircut for the occasion. The vouchers offer a 25% discount, but only if over 100 students take up the offer. One hundred and seven students decide to get their haircut. The salon charges $45 per cut.

a What is the total cost for the 107 students before using the '25% off' voucher?

Answer:

---

b By how much does the voucher reduce the cost?

Answer:

---

c What is the final cost for the whole group of 107 students?

Answer:

Unit 13: Deals

QUESTION 1

A shop sells a bottle of shampoo for $14.50 each or two for $26.

a Which is the better deal and why?

Answer:

_____

b How much is the price difference per bottle?

Answer:

_____

QUESTION 2

A store sells mousse for $8.95 per bottle or two for $15.

a Which is the better buy?

Answer:

_____

b How much is the difference per bottle?

Answer:

_____

QUESTION 3

A hair care store has an offer for customers to buy one bottle of conditioner for $12.50 or three bottles of the same product for $40.

a Which is the better deal?

Answer:

_____

_____

b How much is the difference?

Answer:

_____

QUESTION 4

A store offers customers a hair care product for $7.95 or 'buy two get one free' for $22. Which is the better buy and why?

Answer:

_____

_____

_____

QUESTION 5

A customer wants to buy hair colour and a store has an offer of one bottle for $11.95 or 'buy one get one free' for $23. Which is the better deal and why?

Answer:

_____

_____

_____

QUESTION 6

A shop has an offer where a customer can get a free bottle of shampoo worth $15, if they spend over $50. Another shop offers two free bottles of the same shampoo, if the customer spends over $85. Which shop would you spend your money in and why?

Answer:

_____

_____

_____

_____

QUESTION 7

A store has a special whereby if a customer spends $50 they will receive a $10 voucher to purchase more goods at the same store. If a customer spends $200, how much money in vouchers could they expect to receive?

Answer:

_____

QUESTION 8

A store offers a special whereby if a customer spends $100 they will receive a $15 voucher. A customer purchases over $300 of goods. How much money in vouchers could they expect to receive?

Answer:

_____

QUESTION 9

A salon offers shaving kits for $49.95 during the mid-year sale. A customer purchases three as gifts and pays for them with 2 × $100 notes. What change is given?

Answer:

_____

QUESTION 10

Hair care products are on sale whereby if a customer purchases two jars of hair gel for $19.95, they will get a third jar free. The customer decides to purchase six jars of the product. How many will they end up with in total, considering the offer?

Answer:

_____

Hairdressing
Practice Written Exam
for the Hairdressing Trade

Reading time: 10 minutes

Writing time: 1 hour 30 minutes

Section A: Literacy

Section B: General Mathematics

Section C: Trade Mathematics

QUESTION and ANSWER BOOK

Section	Topic	Number of questions	Marks
A	Literacy	7	23
B	General Mathematics	11	25
C	Trade Mathematics	34	52
		Total 52	Total 100

The sections may be completed in the order of your choice.

NO CALCULATORS are to be used during the exam.

Spelling

Read the passage below and then underline the 20 spelling errors.

10 marks

> Gabrielle and Lakkari entered a hair salon and desided to have diferent
> styles. It was the end of the shoping day and they were keen to spoill
> themselves after a hard day in the speciallty shops. Gabrielle chose
> to have a semi-colour and Lakkari settled on having full-head foils.
> Normaly, the salon would be very bussy but the girls were lucky that
> there had been only a few bokings on this day. Everyone was exsited.
>
> One hairdreser placed a cape over Lakkari and began to prapare her
> hair for the foyles. The hairdresser was happry to have a chat and
> explaned to Lakkari that she had a busy weakend planned. Meenwhile,
> Gabrielle was tended to by the other hairdresser who was also a keen
> convasationalist. Gabrielle had decided that she wanted a blue rince as
> her hair colour and the hairdresser agreed that this would be a great
> look! Everything went acording to plan and the results turned out to be
> wonderfull. Both Gabrielle and Lakkari had enjoyed their visit to the
> salon and each was sporting different and stylish looks.

Correct the spelling errors by writing them out with the correct spelling below.

_____

_____

Alphabetising

Put the following words into alphabetical order.

7 marks

regrowth	streaks
customer	braiding
service	tinting
half-head foils	voucher
comb-over	colour correction
blow-dry	thinning scissors
dimensional lift	human hair mannequin

_____

_____

_____

_____

_____

_____

_____

_____

_____

_____

_____

_____

_____

_____

_____

Comprehension

Short-answer questions

Specific instructions to students

- Read the following passage and answer the questions below.

Paul and Maria started work at the local hair salon centre at 9.00 a.m. on a Thursday. There was late-night shopping and both knew it was going to be a long day as one of the other hairdressers had called in ill. Thursday nights were always popular for families and students and, with students going back to school in a week, Paul felt that this could be one of their busiest working days. He decided to ring Jamie and ask him to help out. Unfortunately, Jamie was unavailable as he was travelling to Melbourne for the weekend. Luckily, Amber was available and left for the salon straightaway, arriving at 9.25 a.m. Soon after, the first customers began to arrive. Paul's first customer was a man who required a style cut. Maria's first customer was a young lady who had short hair and wanted a half-head of foils. Amber's first customer arrived less than 5 minutes later and the customer wanted a wash, cut and blow-dry.

By midday, everything had been moving along smoothly. Paul had completed eight style cuts, Maria had been kept busy with working on foils as well as putting a semi-colour through two women's hair and Amber had completed nine wash, cut and blow-dry treatments. Paul took his lunch break first, followed by Maria then Amber. They needed to stagger the breaks so that there were at least two hairdressers in the salon at all times. The rest of the day was very prosperous for the salon. By close, the salon had takings in the till well over the norm for a Thursday's trading. Paul was so excited that he shouted dinner and drinks for Maria and Amber at a local restaurant.

QUESTION 1   1 mark

What time did the salon open on the Thursday?

Answer:

_____

QUESTION 2   1 mark

Why did Paul feel that this was going to be one of their busiest days?

Answer:

_____

_____

QUESTION 3   1 mark

What did each hairdresser's first customer want as their hair treatment?

Answer:

_____

_____

_____

QUESTION 4   1 mark

By midday, what treatments had each hairdresser completed?

Answer:

_____

_____

_____

_____

QUESTION 5   2 marks

Why did Paul choose to stagger their breaks?

Answer:

_____

_____

Section B: General Mathematics

QUESTION 1   1 + 1 + 1 = 3 marks

What unit of measurement would you use to measure:

a   the length of a hair extension?

Answer:

_____

b   the temperature of a steriliser?

Answer:

_____

c   the amount of hair colour?

Answer:

_____

QUESTION 2   1 + 1 + 1 = 3 marks

Write an example of the following and give an instance of where it may be found in the hairdressing industry:

a   percentages

Answer:

_____

b   decimals

Answer:

_____

c   fractions

Answer:

_____

QUESTION 3   1 + 1 = 2 marks

Convert the following units:

a   1 kg to grams

Answer:

_____

b   1500 g to kilograms

Answer:

_____

QUESTION 4   1 mark
Write the following in descending order:

0.7   0.71   7.1   70.1   701.00   7.0

Answer:

_____

QUESTION 5   1 + 1 = 2 marks
Write the decimal number that is between the
following:

a   0.1 and 0.2

Answer:

_____

b   1.3 and 1.4

Answer:

_____

QUESTION 6   1 + 1 = 2 marks
Round off the following numbers to two decimal
places:

a   5.177

Answer:

_____

b   12.655

Answer:

_____

QUESTION 7   1 + 1 = 2 marks
Estimate the following by approximation:

a $101 \times 81 =$

Answer:

_____

b $399 \times 21 =$

Answer:

_____

QUESTION 8   1 + 1 = 2 marks
What do the following add up to?

a $25, $13.50 and $165.50

Answer:

_____

b $4, $5.99 and $229.50

Answer:

_____

QUESTION 9   1 + 1 = 2 marks
Subtract the following:

a   196 from 813

Answer:

_____

b   5556 from 9223

Answer:

_____

QUESTION 10   1 + 1 = 2 marks
Use division to solve:

a $4824 \div 3 =$

Answer:

_____

b $84.2 \div 0.4 =$

Answer:

_____

QUESTION 11   2 + 2 = 4 marks
Using BODMAS, solve:

a $(3 \times 7) \times 4 + 9 - 5 =$

Answer:

_____

b $(8 \times 12) \times 2 + 8 - 4 =$

Answer:

_____

Section C: Trade Mathematics

Basic Operations

Addition

QUESTION 1   1 mark

A salon purchases 36 bottles of shampoo, 144 capes or gowns and 15 skeleton brushes. How many items have been purchased in total?

Answer:

QUESTION 2   1 mark

A hairdresser completes three cuts charging $25, $45 and $17. How much has been charged in total?

Answer:

Subtraction

QUESTION 1   1 mark

A salon uses 57 foils from a box that contains 150 foils. How many remain?

Answer:

QUESTION 2   1 mark

A customer purchases hair care products and the total comes to $124. The manager takes off a discount of $35 during a sale. How much does the customer pay?

Answer:

Multiplication

QUESTION 1   1 mark

A salon purchases four deluxe salon stools for $124 each, two shampoo basins for $635 each and 3 mannequins heads costing $32 each. What is the total cost?

Answer:

QUESTION 2   1 mark

A salon purchases 5.5 inch hairdressing scissors with cases. If one pair costs $23, how much will eight pairs cost?

Answer:

Division

QUESTION 1   1 mark

The week's takings for a salon are $3155. If the salon was open for six days, what would be the average takings per day?

Answer:

QUESTION 2   1 mark

At a yearly stocktake at a salon, a store person counts 72 bottles of conditioner. If 12 bottles are packed into each box, how many boxes are there?

Answer:

Decimals

Addition

QUESTION 1   1 mark

A family buys the following hair care products from a store: a can of hair spray for $19.95, a tinting bowl for $9.50 and a set of hair brushes for $34.50. How much for the purchases in total?

Answer:

QUESTION 2   1 mark

A salon has customers who need style cuts in the lead-up to the festive season. The cost for one cut is $39.50, another is $43.50 and a third cut is $21.50. How much is the total for all three?

Answer:

Subtraction

An apprentice works 38 hours and earns $418.50. He spends $55.95 on clothes and $25.00 on a mobile phone recharge card. How much is left?

Answer:

QUESTION 2   1 mark

A three-bar footrest is purchased for a salon at a cost of $24.50. If it is paid for with a $50 note from the float, how much change will be given?

Answer:

Multiplication

QUESTION 1   1 + 1 = 2 marks

A hairdresser goes to a sale where jars of hair coating cream are priced at $49.95.

a   How much does it cost for three jars?

Answer:

b   What is the change from $150?

Answer:

QUESTION 2   1 + 1 = 2 marks

Four hairdressing equipment trolleys are purchased at a cost of $148.50 each.

a   What is the total of this purchase?

Answer:

b   What is the change from $600.00?

Answer:

Division

QUESTION 1   1 mark

A salon has takings of $1455.00 over 12 hours for a Thursday's trading. How much does this work out to be, on average, per hour?

Answer:

QUESTION 2   2 marks

Four people have style cuts. The total for all four customers comes to $76.80. What is the cost to each customer, assuming they all have the same cut?

Answer:

Fractions

QUESTION 1   1 mark

$\frac{1}{4} + \frac{1}{2} =$

Answer:

QUESTION 2   1 mark

$\frac{4}{5} - \frac{1}{3} =$

Answer:

QUESTION 3   1 mark

$\frac{2}{3} \times \frac{1}{4} =$

Answer:

QUESTION 4   1 mark

$\frac{3}{4} \div \frac{1}{2} =$

Answer:

Percentages

QUESTION 1   1 + 1 = 2 marks

A salon has a '10% off' sale on all items. If a customer purchases items totalling $149, what is the final sale price?

Answer:

QUESTION 2   1 + 1 + 1 = 3 marks

Hair care products are discounted by 20%. The regular retail price of certain products comes to $120.

a   How much is the discount worth?

Answer:

_____

b   What is the price of the products after the discount?

Answer:

_____

c   How much change would be needed if a $100 note was used to pay for the products?

Answer:

_____

Measurement Conversions

QUESTION 1   2 marks

How many grams are there in 1.85 kg?

Answer:

_____

QUESTION 2   2 marks

35 mm converts to how many centimetres?

Answer:

_____

Area

QUESTION 1   2 marks

The floor area of a salon measures 15 m by 6 m. What is the total floor area?

Answer:

_____

QUESTION 2   2 marks

What is the total window area that measures 2.2 m by 1.5 m and displays hair care products?

Answer:

_____

Earning Wages

QUESTION 1   2 marks

A part-time hairdresser gets paid $12.50 per hour. If he works 15 hours a week, how much will be his gross pay?

Answer:

_____

QUESTION 2   2 marks

A hairdresser spends the following time on five different customers: 17 minutes, 35 minutes, 19 minutes, 48 minutes and 58 minutes respectively.

a   How much time, in minutes, has been taken?

Answer:

_____

b   How much time, in hours and minutes, has been taken?

Answer:

_____

Squaring Numbers

QUESTION 1   2 marks

What is 7^2?

Answer:

_____

QUESTION 2   2 marks

The floor area of a warehouse measures 13 m × 13 m. What is the total floor area?

Answer:

_____

Vouchers

QUESTION 1   2 marks

A customer walks into a salon with a '20% off' voucher. If $148.60 worth of products are purchased, what will be the final cost to the customer once the voucher is used?

Answer:

_____

QUESTION 2   2 marks

A customer purchases goods to the total of $78.60. A voucher for '15% off' is then produced. How much is charged after the voucher is used?

Answer:

_____

Deals

QUESTION 1   2 marks

A store has bottles of shampoo on special for $14.95, or you can buy two for $26. Which is the better deal and how much, if any, will be saved?

Answer:

_____

_____

QUESTION 2   2 marks

A store sells a bottle of mousse for $9.50 or three for $27. Which is the better deal and how much, if any, will be saved?

Answer:

_____

_____

_____

Glossary

Bob cut   Classic look of the 1950s and 1960s. The style is short and straight but blow-dried and curled under.

Conditioner   Creamy hair product meant to be used after shampoo. Moisturises and detangles hair.

Feathering   A cutting technique hairdressers use to take hard lines out of the hair. By cutting into the hair, soft lines can be created.

Foils   A highlighting method that incorporates selecting strands of hair and applying colour to add visual interest to hair.

Fringe   The front section of hair that creates a frame for your face; can be one of the most important parts of a hairstyle.

Gown   Lightweight, waterproof, adjustable, protective item that is placed over the front of the customer and adjusted around the neck.

Graduation   The build up of a shape. It can create a curve in the hair and is the opposite of layering.

Hair extensions   Pieces of real or synthetic hair weaved close to the scalp in order to achieve greater length and/or fullness.

Layering   A technique used by hairdressers to make hair appear thinner or thicker.

Make over   Total change of style.

Mousse   An aerosol foam used in hair styling.

Perm   Curls, generally long-lasting, created by restructuring the hair molecules with a chemical or heat treatment.

Semi-permanent   A colour which lasts from 6–8 shampoos.

Streaks   A colouring process for particular strands of hair that can give your hair brighter effects and add volume to certain types of hair.

Texturiser   A treatment left on the hair for a short period of time that slightly relaxes the natural curl of hair.

Tint   Enriches a natural hair colour and is less harsh than other colouring techniques. Usually washes out after 5–8 weeks.

Tint brush   Used to apply tints from a bowl.

Treatment   Used between shampoo and conditioner to put protein back into hair.

Wefts   Temporary hair extensions which are glued into your hair.

Formulae and Data

Circumference of a Circle

$C = \pi \times d$

where: C = circumference, π = 3.14, d = diameter

Diameter of a Circle

$d = \dfrac{C}{\pi}$

Where: C = circumference, π = 3.14, d = diameter

Area

$A = l \times b$

Area = length × breadth and is given in square units

Volume of a Cube

$V = l \times w \times h$

Volume = length × width × height and is given in cubic units

Volume of a Cylinder

$V_c = \pi \times r^2 \times h$

Where: V_c = volume of a cylinder, π = 3.14, r = radius, h = height

Times Tables

1

1 × 1	=	1
2 × 1	=	2
3 × 1	=	3
4 × 1	=	4
5 × 1	=	5
6 × 1	=	6
7 × 1	=	7
8 × 1	=	8
9 × 1	=	9
10 × 1	=	10
11 × 1	=	11
12 × 1	=	12

2

1 × 2	=	2
2 × 2	=	4
3 × 2	=	6
4 × 2	=	8
5 × 2	=	10
6 × 2	=	12
7 × 2	=	14
8 × 2	=	16
9 × 2	=	18
10 × 2	=	20
11 × 2	=	22
12 × 2	=	24

3

1 × 3	=	3
2 × 3	=	6
3 × 3	=	9
4 × 3	=	12
5 × 3	=	15
6 × 3	=	18
7 × 3	=	21
8 × 3	=	24
9 × 3	=	27
10 × 3	=	30
11 × 3	=	33
12 × 3	=	36

4

1 × 4	=	4
2 × 4	=	8
3 × 4	=	12
4 × 4	=	16
5 × 4	=	20
6 × 4	=	24
7 × 4	=	28
8 × 4	=	32
9 × 4	=	36
10 × 4	=	40
11 × 4	=	44
12 × 4	=	48

5

1 × 5	=	5
2 × 5	=	10
3 × 5	=	15
4 × 5	=	20
5 × 5	=	25
6 × 5	=	30
7 × 5	=	35
8 × 5	=	40
9 × 5	=	45
10 × 5	=	50
11 × 5	=	55
12 × 5	=	60

6

1 × 6	=	6
2 × 6	=	12
3 × 6	=	18
4 × 6	=	24
5 × 6	=	30
6 × 6	=	36
7 × 6	=	42
8 × 6	=	48
9 × 6	=	54
10 × 6	=	60
11 × 6	=	66
12 × 6	=	72

7

1 × 7	=	7
2 × 7	=	14
3 × 7	=	21
4 × 7	=	28
5 × 7	=	35
6 × 7	=	42
7 × 7	=	49
8 × 7	=	56
9 × 7	=	63
10 × 7	=	70
11 × 7	=	77
12 × 7	=	84

8

1 × 8	=	8
2 × 8	=	16
3 × 8	=	24
4 × 8	=	32
5 × 8	=	40
6 × 8	=	48
7 × 8	=	56
8 × 8	=	64
9 × 8	=	72
10 × 8	=	80
11 × 8	=	88
12 × 8	=	96

9

1 × 9	=	9
2 × 9	=	18
3 × 9	=	27
4 × 9	=	36
5 × 9	=	45
6 × 9	=	54
7 × 9	=	63
8 × 9	=	72
9 × 9	=	81
10 × 9	=	90
11 × 9	=	99
12 × 9	=	108

10

1 × 10	=	10
2 × 10	=	20
3 × 10	=	30
4 × 10	=	40
5 × 10	=	50
6 × 10	=	60
7 × 10	=	70
8 × 10	=	80
9 × 10	=	90
10 × 10	=	100
11 × 10	=	110
12 × 10	=	120

11

1 × 11	=	11
2 × 11	=	22
3 × 11	=	33
4 × 11	=	44
5 × 11	=	55
6 × 11	=	66
7 × 11	=	77
8 × 11	=	88
9 × 11	=	99
10 × 11	=	110
11 × 11	=	121
12 × 11	=	132

12

1 × 12	=	12
2 × 12	=	24
3 × 12	=	36
4 × 12	=	48
5 × 12	=	60
6 × 12	=	72
7 × 12	=	84
8 × 12	=	96
9 × 12	=	108
10 × 12	=	120
11 × 12	=	132
12 × 12	=	144

9780170462839

Multiplication Grid

	1	2	3	4	5	6	7	8	9	10	11	12
1	1	2	3	4	5	6	7	8	9	10	11	12
2	2	4	6	8	10	12	14	16	18	20	22	24
3	3	6	9	12	15	18	21	24	27	30	33	36
4	4	8	12	16	20	24	28	32	36	40	44	48
5	5	10	15	20	25	30	35	40	45	50	55	60
6	6	12	18	24	30	36	42	48	54	60	66	72
7	7	14	21	28	35	42	49	56	63	70	77	84
8	8	16	24	32	40	48	56	64	72	80	88	96
9	9	18	27	36	45	54	63	72	81	90	99	108
10	10	20	30	40	50	60	70	80	90	100	110	120
11	11	22	33	44	55	66	77	88	99	110	121	132
12	12	24	36	48	60	72	84	96	108	120	132	144

Notes

Notes

Notes

9780170462839